A WOMAN
of BLESSING

6 studies for individuals
or groups

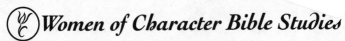

Juanita Ryan

Introductions by Linda Shands

With Guidelines for Leaders
and Study Notes

 Women of Character Bible Studies

IVP

InterVarsity Press
Downers Grove, Illinois
Leicester, England

InterVarsity Press
P. O. Box 1400, Downers Grove, IL 60515, USA
38 De Montfort Street, Leicester LE1 7GP, England

InterVarsity Press® is the book-publishing division of InterVarsity Christian Fellowship®, a student movement active on campus at hundreds of universities, colleges and schools of nursing in the United States of America, and a member movement of the International Fellowship of Evangelical Students. For information about local and regional activities, write Public Relations Dept., InterVarsity Christian Fellowship, 6400 Schroeder Rd., P.O. Box 7895, Madison, WI 53707-7895.

Inter-Varsity Press, UK, is the book-publishing division of the Universities and Colleges Christian Fellowship (formerly the Inter-Varsity Fellowship), a student movement linking Christian Unions in universities and colleges throughout the United Kingdom and the Republic or Ireland, and a member movement of the International Fellowship of Evangelical Students. For information about local and national activities write to UCCF, 38 De Montfort Street, Leicester LE1 7GP.

USA ISBN 0-8308-2043-4

Printed in the United States of America ∞

Contents

Cast of Characters

Each introduction takes the perspective of a different character in a continuing story to introduce the theme of each study. Below are the voices behind each introduction.

1 **Jenny Campbell**—wife and mother in the process of a major move

2 **Joyce**—Jenny's mother-in-law

3 **Alicia**—Coworker of Jenny's spouse, Jack

4 **Ardice**—Jenny's next door neighbor

5 **Karen**—Jenny's best friend

6 **Irene**—Jenny's mother

Other characters

Jack Campbell—Jenny's spouse

Carol—coworker of Jack's and friend of Alicia

Joe—Karen's spouse

Danny and Tommy—Jenny's children

Maggie—Jenny's neighbor and friend of Ardice

Introducing *A Woman of Blessing*

Every Sunday in the church where we worship, the children are called to the front before they leave for their class so we as a congregation can stretch out our hands and bless them. I am always moved by this simple act. Sometimes I am moved to tears. Sometimes to smiles. But this simple act of blessing is always a deeply joyous thing. In this act I am able to express my affection and valuing for these little ones. I am reminded that they are good gifts from God. I am reminded of God's love for them, and for me.

Every week I meet with friends who pray for me and for whom I pray. We pray for God's care and provision in each other's lives in very specific ways. I feel loved. And valued. I am blessed. And I feel able to express my love and gratitude for them as I bless them.

The act of blessing is an act of love. It acknowledges and strengthens our spiritual connection with each other. It expresses our concern and gratitude and valuing of each other.

Sometimes blessing is expressed in prayer. But blessing is also expressed in words of affirmation. In acts of kindness. In celebrating. In the clapping of hands. In letters of recognition and gratitude. In worship.

The story in this study shows us the place of blessing and of being a blessing in the life of a woman named Jenny who experiences the difficulty of leaving the area that has always been home to her to relocate in a distant place. As Jenny's life weaves in and out of the lives of other women both near and far, she is blessed and she becomes a blessing—through prayers, phone calls, index cards, invitations, letters, warm cookies and visits.

These studies are designed to draw you into the act of blessing and the experience of being blessed. Blessing and being blessed require that we grow in our awareness and sensitivity to others and their needs, that we reach out in love, that we open our hearts to receive from others, that we are on the lookout for good gifts from God, that we are ready to celebrate each gift —each blessing—as it comes.

May your joy increase as God continues to bless you and make you a woman of blessing.

Suggestions for Individual Study

1. As you begin each study pray that God will speak to you through his Word.

2. Read the introduction to the study, "Setting the Stage," and respond to the questions that follow it. The story is designed to draw you into the topic at hand and help you begin to see how the Scripture relates to daily life. If there will be a week or more between your studies, then you may want to read all of the introductions in one sitting to get the flow of the ongoing story. This will help if you find that you are having trouble keeping track of all the characters.

3. This is an inductive Bible study, designed to help you discover for yourself what Scripture is saying. Each study deals with a particular passage—so that you can really delve into the author's meaning in that context. Read and reread the passage to be studied. The questions are written using the language of the New International Version, so you may wish to use that version of the Bible. The New Revised Standard Version is also recommended.

4. "God's Word for Us" includes three types of questions. *Observation* questions ask about the basic facts: who, what, when, where and how. *Interpretation* questions delve into the meaning of the passage. *Application* questions (also found in the "Now or Later" section) help you discover the implications of the text for growing in Christ. These three keys unlock the treasures of Scripture.

Write your answers to the study questions in the spaces provided or in a personal journal. Writing can bring clarity and deeper understanding of yourself and of God's Word.

5. Use the study notes at the back of the guide to gain additional insight and information after you have worked through the questions for yourself.

6. Move to the "Now or Later" section. These are ideas for you to freely use in closing your study and responding to God. You may want to choose one of these to do right away and continue working through the other ideas on subsequent days to reinforce what you are learning.

Suggestions for Members of a Group Study

1. Come to the study prepared. Follow the suggestions for individual study mentioned above. You will find that careful preparation will greatly enrich your time spent in group discussion.

2. Be willing to participate in the discussion. The leader of your group will not be lecturing. Instead, she will be encouraging the members of the group to discuss what they have learned. The leader will be asking the questions that are found in this guide.

3. Stick to the topic being discussed. Your answers should be based on the verses which are the focus of the discussion and not on outside authorities such as commentaries or speakers. These studies focus on a particular passage of Scripture. Only rarely should you refer to other portions of the Bible. This allows for everyone to participate on equal ground and for in-depth study.

4. Be sensitive to the other members of the group. Listen attentively when they describe what they have learned. You may be surprised by their insights! Each question assumes a variety of answers. Many questions do not have "right" answers, particularly questions that aim at meaning or application. Instead the questions push us to explore the passage more thoroughly.

When possible, link what you say to the comments of others. Also, be affirming whenever you can. This will encourage some of the more hesitant members of the group to participate.

5. Be careful not to dominate the discussion. We are sometimes so eager to express our thoughts that we leave too little opportunity for others to respond. By all means participate! But allow others to also.

6. Expect God to teach you through the passage being discussed and through the other members of the group. Pray that you will have an enjoyable and profitable time together, but also that as a result of the study, you will find ways that you can take action individually and/or as a group.

7. It will be helpful for groups to follow a few basic guidelines. These guidelines, which you may wish to adapt to your situation, should be read at the beginning of the first session.

☐ Anything said in the group is considered confidential and will not be discussed outside the group unless specific permission is given to do so.

☐ We will provide time for each person present to talk if he or she feels comfortable doing so.

☐ We will talk about ourselves and our own situations, avoiding conversation about other people.

☐ We will listen attentively to each other.

☐ We will be very cautious about giving advice.

☐ We will pray for each other.

8. If you are the group leader, you will find additional suggestions at the back of the guide.

1

Called to Be Blessed and to Be a Blessing

Genesis 12:1-5

 SETTING THE STAGE:

Jenny's Story

June 15—circled on the calendar in red. A year ago today, I had clutched the iron railing on the observatory platform peering down to where the city should have been. Smog had settled in thick brown wads around Hyatt Towers cutting off the Tri-met building at the fortieth floor, completely obliterating the web of freeway below. Even as I inhaled warm mountain breeze, I could taste the noxious fumes.

When we were young, we'd breathed flower-scented air: jasmine in the summer, lilac in the spring. By the time we got married and had children of our own, even the suburban skies were clogged with pollution. Still, that city had always been our home.

I shivered, remembering the phone call. It had come right at Danny's bedtime with the bathtub overflowing and abandoned toys strewn across the kitchen floor.

"Two weeks?" I don't remember screeching, at least not out loud, but the telephone line went silent. I know now he was trying to digest my hysteria, deciding how to respond.

"What's wrong? I thought you'd be glad to get out of that apartment. You can breathe here, Jenny. You should see the trees." His voice grew louder, drowning out my sobs. "I got the job in a day! They liked my work so much they hired me on the spot. Found a house too. It's the Ritz compared to Steel Street, and half the rent. We can get the kids a dog."

A dog? Did he think a dog could take the place of family and lifelong friends?

"It's the chance of a lifetime." I can still hear his voice thick with disappointment. "I thought you'd be happy for me."

I flicked a flake of chipped brown paint off the rail and thought of hot cement and cool grass beneath bare feet. Huge maple trees, roots buckling the sidewalk, that sheltered Kool-Aid stands and sunburnt skin. Neighborhood games of hide and seek. Thick green pop bottles buried under slivered ice. Spitting watermelon seeds, then later watching Daddy dig the shoots out of the grass.

I thought of gully-washer rains that overflowed the gutters while cement rivers channeled muddy water to the sea. Running two blocks from the school bus stop. Mama waiting at the door with a towel and a worried frown. "You'll catch pneumonia." Chocolate chip cookies melting on my tongue while a pan of cocoa simmered on the stove.

In a few hours we would leave it all behind.

I stepped back as people spilled from the Planetarium onto the observatory platform. The second show was over and my family would be waiting in the car, still wondering, I'm sure, why I'd insisted we come.

How can he do this so easily? He grew up here too. Mom and Daddy, Karen and Joe. His own parents for pete's sake. Inside my chest, fear and anger wrestled for first prize. New job or no, a thousand miles was just too far.

Somehow cupboards had been emptied, boxes filled. The children excited and cranky by turns as strangers carted away the washing machine, Tommy's high chair, Danny's crib. "You're a big boy now. We'll get you a real bed."

So little time to say goodbye.

"We'll see you soon."

"Wild horses couldn't keep us away."

"Can we pitch a tent in your backyard?" Forced laughter, awkward hugs.

I rubbed the damp from underneath my eyes. *Great. Now I have mascara all over my face. He'll know I've been crying.*

A year ago today.

I wish I could have seen into the future—caught a glimpse of the joy. Maybe it wouldn't have been so hard. Then again, I think that nothing would have helped. It had simply been my time for tears.

---

1. God certainly had many rich blessings in store for Jenny and her family in the move they faced. But first Jenny needed to grieve and let go in order to be open to receive those blessings. Why is this often an important first step in receiving blessing from God?

When have you experienced a time of grieving and letting go which prepared you to be open to receive God's blessings for you?

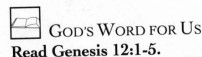 GOD'S WORD FOR US

Read Genesis 12:1-5.

2. What promises does God make to Abram (later called *Abraham*) in this text?

How would you restate these promises in your own words?

3. We receive much of God's blessing in our lives simply because it is given to us. Sometimes, however, we are asked by God to be active participants in receiving his blessing. What does God ask Abram to do in order to receive what God has for him?

4. List several ways in which God has blessed you by simply giving to you.

5. Think of a time when God asked you to actively participate in receiving a blessing he had for you. What happened?

6. What factors would have made Abram's journey complicated (vv. 4-5)?

7. Despite the difficulties, what benefits come to us when we are active participants in receiving God's blessing?

8. God tells Abram not only that he wants to bless him but that he wants to make him a blessing to others. List some of the ways all the peoples of the earth have been blessed through Abram.

9. How would you describe the relationship between being blessed by God and being a blessing to others?

10. How have you seen this relationship between being blessed and being a blessing work in your own life?

 Now or Later

Ideas to close your group meeting or personal study or for continued daily reflection.

☐ Spend some time reflecting and praying about the following questions:

We are not all called to the same task, or even blessed in the same ways. What are some of the ways God has been blessing you?

What do you think God is saying to you about how he wants to continue to bless you?

What do you think God is saying to you about the ways he wants to make you a blessing to others?

How is God asking you to participate in receiving the blessings he has for you and in being a blessing to others?

☐ Write a prayer of thanksgiving for the ways God has blessed you and is blessing you.

☐ Write a prayer asking for wisdom and strength to be willing to participate in God's plan to continue to bless you and to make you a blessing to others.

☐ Read and reflect on 2 Corinthians 5:18-19.

2

Receiving Blessing from God

Psalm 84

 SETTING THE STAGE:

Joyce's Story

"Oh, Joyce, I told myself I wasn't going to cry."

I squeezed Irene's shoulder and handed her the box of Kleenex. "You might as well tell a mosquito not to bite. It'll ignore you every time."

She tried a laugh. It sounded like someone had stepped on a frog. "You're so funny. I know I shouldn't carry on like this, but it's hard. I can't believe they're gone."

"Well, they are." I reached for the last tissue in the box, picked up my cup of lukewarm Sanka then pushed it away. "What's worse; they took our grandsons with them . . . how do you drink this stuff?"

I could have kicked myself.

"Oh, dear, has the jar gone bad? I keep it for company. I can only have hot water and herb tea—one dunk."

Jenny's mother is the closest thing to a saint I'll ever meet. We have nothing in common except for our children's marriage and our God. It makes for a wonderful friendship.

I remember little else about that day. Just our conversation and the sight of my son's powder blue Camero disappearing around the corner. I tried convincing myself it wouldn't be so bad. "We can take turns visiting at Christmas," I told Irene, "And think of the summer vacations we'll have." It wasn't working for either of us.

Jenny wrote faithfully every week. Her letters to her mother were full of news: *The boys and I picked blackberries today. Tommy loves his new two wheeler. It stays light here until almost ten o'clock!* But most of the ones addressed to me had an I'm-so-lonely-I-can't-handle-this theme.

At first it hurt my feelings. Then I realized I should be grateful that Jenny trusted me enough to be honest. She obviously didn't want to worry her mother. My shoulders were broader — in every sense of the word.

One thing for sure, her letters drove me to my knees. I knew God had a plan for them, I just didn't know the what's, when's and why's. *Why did they have to move so far away? Are we a part of the plan?*

You are.

The message, wherever it came from was loud and clear. So was the idea that jolted me from sleep at 3:00 a.m.

I pawed through the junk drawer and came up with an unopened package of 3 × 5's and several colored pens, three of which actually produced ink. By the time Howard's Drugstore opened at 9:00, I had a stack of neatly printed cards.

The only tin boxes I could find were covered with butterflies or frilly flowers. Ugh. But I was too excited to try another store. I chose the flowers and a package of stickers to match — overkill, but if it worked . . .

The final product didn't turn out half bad. I printed the

label in neon orange—FIVE MINUTE BLESSINGS—placed the cards inside, then wrote a short note. JENNY, CHOOSE ONE EACH DAY—SATISFACTION GUARANTEED.

Scan the room; thank God for everything you see. Take a picture of the sunset. Climb a hill. Close your eyes and feel the wind. Eat an ice cream cone. Count the stars. See how high you can go in Danny's swing. Ride Tommy's bike. Pick dandelions, and put them in a jar. Stand in the rain. Bake cookies for a neighbor. Sing "Amazing Grace."

I included lots of hymns—there were a lot of cards to fill. Three-hundred-sixty-five exercises in happiness. I wasn't sure if they'd help Jenny, but I hadn't felt so good in years.

---

1. As we will see in this psalm, an important aspect of receiving blessing from God is to heighten our awareness of his presence in our lives. How might Joyce's gift to Jenny help Jenny receive God's blessings?

 GOD'S WORD FOR US
Read Psalm 84.

---

2. According to verses 1-4, the psalmist experiences God's presence in an especially powerful way in the temple, the place of worship. How does he describe it?

Where do you experience God's presence?

3. According to verses 1-2, what does the writer experience of being away from God's presence?

4. Verses 4-7 promise a blessing for those whose "strength is in [God]" and for those "who set their hearts on a pilgrimage." What do you see as the meaning of each of these metaphors?

5. What blessings are promised (vv. 6-7)?

How would you restate these promises in your own words?

6. The writer then asks for God's attention and blessing (vv. 8-9). Rewrite this as a prayer for God's attention and blessing in your own life, making it as specific as you like.

---

7. How does the writer describe God in verses 10-12?

---

8. The final phrase makes a direct link between trusting God and receiving God's blessing. How would you describe the relationship between trusting God and receiving God's blessing from your own experience?

 NOW OR LATER

☐ Make a list of the blessings you receive when you are in God's presence.

☐ What might you do this week to experience God's presence and to receive his blessing?

☐ What activities help you to grow in your trust of God? Make a plan to participate in one such activity this week.

☐ Read and reflect on Psalm 103.

3

Receiving Blessing from God's Family

Ephesians 4:1-16

 SETTING THE STAGE:

Alicia's Story

Cracked crab and beer around a campfire at Agate Beach; a company tradition held sacred by employer and employees alike. Most of them, anyway. A few of us go only because it's expected—like working overtime or chipping in for a bottle on the boss's birthday. I always offer to buy the card instead.

It was pitch black away from the fire. A mini-gale threw fist-fuls of sand into our faces as Carol and I picked our way across the shell-littered beach toward the Seaward Gift Shop and Restaurant in search of diet soda.

"I wouldn't mind a hotdog either," I yelled in Carol's ear.

She grabbed my arm and pulled me toward the lighted window. "Or a sit-down dinner . . ."

I followed her pointing finger. *So that's where they went.* The new guy Jack Campbell, his wife, Jenny, and their two little boys were seated in a corner booth eating hamburgers and potato salad. Jack looked glum and

Jenny stared down at her plate.

"Too good for us, Alicia," Carol whispered as we searched the freezer for our choice of drink.

I shook my head. "Maybe they don't like crab."

"So? I don't either, but at least I sit with the others."

I let the remark pass. But Monday at work she was at it again. "Jack's friendly enough. In fact he's kind of cute. But she didn't say boo the entire night. I say she's stuck on herself."

I remembered Jenny's warm hello when we were introduced, her tentative smile when someone looked her way, and instantly felt ashamed. "You know, none of us exactly went out of our way to make her welcome. I think she's just shy. And lonely too, I'll bet. They've only been here two weeks."

Carol laughed. "Okay, Ms. Welcome Wagon. Why don't you invite her to one of those Bible wingdings of yours? The one you're always trying to con me into."

"What a great idea! I'll call her tonight."

Carol rolled her eyes. "Oh brother. Bet you a hot fudge sundae she doesn't go."

I grinned. "You're on. But make it two. Jenny joins us if I win."

The phone call was harder to make than I'd thought. My first-grader had the flu. The washing machine broke down and I had to rinse out underwear by hand. By Sunday it was all I could do to drag myself to church. It wasn't until they announced the topic of Monday evening's study that I remembered Jenny. *I'll call as soon as I get home.*

I tried three times before I got through. "We call our folks on Sunday afternoons." I could tell she'd been crying.

"Uh, maybe this isn't a good time?"

"Oh, no. It's fine. Jack's watching the ballgame and the kids are taking naps. It's nice to have someone to talk to."

An hour later I'd discovered we shared a love for gardening, mystery novels and family camping trips. "But I don't think we'll try the beach again," she confided. "The wind makes Danny's asthma act up and I'm allergic to crab."

"We'll have to take you to the high lakes in August. In the meantime would you settle for a Bible study on Monday night?"

"Oh, Alicia, I would love that. I . . . I've been praying for Christian friends."

All right! I stifled a triumphant laugh. "I'll pick you up at 6:30. And if it's all right with you, we'll be going out for ice cream afterwards. Carol's treat."

---

1. What blessing was Jenny needing from God's family?

What specific blessings did Alicia give to Jenny by reaching out to her?

 GOD'S WORD FOR US
Read Ephesians 4:1-16.

---

2. Sometimes God's blessing (care and provision) comes to us through other members of God's family. List the characteristics Paul encourages in believers in verse 2.

How might these qualities lead to a person being a blessing to others?

---

3. The passage goes on to talk about the importance of unity and a sense of connection with others in the community of faith (vv. 3-6). In what ways is a sense of connection with other Christians helpful to you?

---

4. How are you hurt when that sense of connection is lacking?

---

5. Paul explains (vv. 7-13) that the reason we have been gifted to minister to each other is in order to use our gifts to bless each other with increased faith, knowledge and spiritual growth. How has the ministry of other Christians (preaching, teaching, writing, praying, counseling) impacted your life? Give one or two specific examples.

6. In verses 14-16 Paul uses metaphors to describe our need for each other as Christians and the outcome of the blessing we can have in each other's lives. How does Paul describe our need?

7. How does he describe the benefits, or blessing, we can have in each other's lives?

8. The passage tells us that our growth, spiritually, is a direct result of being loved. How are these two realities related in your experience?

9. What blessing (care and provision) do you need from God's family at this time?

NOW OR LATER

☐ Make a list of thank-you notes you might write, to express your gratitude to those who have blessed your life.

☐ What might help you to receive greater blessing from God's family?

Make a plan to do what you can to put yourself in a place of receiving blessing from others in God's family.

☐ Read and reflect on James 5:13-16.

4

....

Being a Blessing to Others

Philippians 4:1-9

 SETTING THE STAGE:

Ardice's Story

I never had been one to take casseroles or cookies and I saw no reason to start. *Let Maggie do it*, I said to myself, *her antenna's been twirling ever since the "For Rent" sign went down.*

"Don't you want to meet them, Ardice? Aren't you just the least bit curious?"

Never could abide a gossip.

All I wanted was a little peace and quiet. What did I get? Boys, that's what. Hooligans for sure, or I missed my guess.

Sure enough, the minute we got a scrap of sun they were at it; whoopin' and hollerin' and tearing up the yard. Didn't their mother know children should be napping that time of day?

I thought I'd seen the worst of it when they kicked that football over the fence and it landed in the garden. Broke the heads off my broccoli. Two minutes later, there goes the doorbell.

"Hi, lady. Can we please have our ball?"

One chance, I thought. "You keep it to yourself, now. Next time it's mine."

Two weeks later I'd kept the ball three times, ignoring the front bell and tossing it over the fence after they'd gone to bed at night. I'm not a thief, but someone had to teach those kids some manners.

Then they got the dog. An insatiable beast—half lion, half gopher. When he wasn't barking loud enough to wake the neighborhood, he was digging holes under the fence. He obviously preferred my yard to theirs. Not that I blamed him, but dogs and I didn't mix. Never could abide the horrid creatures. The day he dug up three tomato plants and my Dainty Bess rose, was the day I'd had enough.

Jenny answered the phone. "I want you to know," I said with as much civility as I could muster, "that I have called the pound to come pick up that animal of yours. And another thing, if your children throw that ball over my fence one more time, I cannot be responsible for its return."

She mumbled an apology, but that wouldn't restore my garden. The dog took off—over the gate this time and down the street. *Good riddance,* I said to myself.

I could hear the children crying. Maggie called to say she'd seen animal control pick up the Campbell's dog and Jack Campbell's Chevy drive by. Did I know what was going on?

I told her to mind her own business.

The neighborhood was quiet for the first time in weeks. I decided to take a nap, but for some reason, I couldn't sleep. I kept hearing those children cry, and picturing Jenny's tired eyes.

When the doorbell rang at nine o'clock the next morning, I was in no mood for company.

Jenny Campbell stood on my porch, a plate of cookies in one hand, a Dainty Bess rose bush in the other. The boys each held a tomato plant in grubby little fists.

I couldn't say a word, but Jenny did. "Ardice, the boys and I want you to know how sorry we are about your plants. And we found another home for Bear. Our yard is just too small for a dog his size."

"He's on a farm," the oldest boy piped up, "and we get to visit him any time we want."

Then the little one pushed forward. "Mamma says if you let us we can help you fix your garden. I can dig real good."

Jenny and I canned a dozen jars of salsa in September. I took some along when Maggie invited me for tea. She said she could hear me singing all the way up the street and could I tell her what was going on? I smiled and handed her a slip from my Dainty Bess.

"Danny's a good digger," I said, "He can plant it for you in the spring."

---

1. What did Jenny communicate in her sensitivity to Ardice?

What makes this kind of response to anger difficult?

GOD'S WORD FOR US
Read Philippians 4:1-9.

2. What do you discover about Paul's relationship with the Philippians from these verses?

3. What is your reaction to the way Paul addresses the believers at Phillipi in verse 1?

4. In your own words, list the behaviors that Paul encourages in the believers in verses 2-5.

5. If you were to follow these instructions, how might each of these behaviors result in others experiencing you as a blessing (as one who cares for them)?

6. Which of these behaviors is especially difficult for you?

What might help you to grow in your ability to behave in this way?

---

7. In verses 6-9 Paul instructs the readers on "the way of peace." What behaviors lead to being at peace, according to this text?

---

8. How might being at peace increase the likelihood of being a blessing to others?

---

9. What person or situation do you know of that needs someone to offer the peace of Christ?

 Now or Later

☐ Reread verses 6-8. Take some time to follow Paul's instructions.

Notice the things that are making you anxious. Talk to God about them.

Tell God what you need.

Thank God for the ways he has and continues to care and provide for you.

Allow God's peace to flow into your heart and mind.

Reflect on the adjectives: true, noble, right, pure, lovely, admirable. What comes to mind? Let yourself spend some time thinking about things that fit this description.

☐ Spend some time listening to God. Ask God to bring people to mind that you might be a blessing to. Ask him what it is you might do for them. Ask him for the courage and strength to follow his will.

☐ Read and reflect on Hebrews 13:1-3.

5

Blessing God Through Thanksgiving

Psalm 98

 SETTING THE STAGE:

Karen's Story

A pair of swallows re-line last year's nest. Three doe nibble on the rich spring grass. The boys come charging down the hill, dogs at their heels, and the deer bound away to breakfast in a safer spot.

Our house is spacious, old, welcoming. New cabinets, fixtures, three coats of paint and earthtone throw-rugs scattered across re-furbished hardwood floors. Home.

"Karen, our rental house is old," Jenny had said in her first letter. "The yard's even smaller than the one back home. We have fields behind us though, with blackberries, wild apple trees, pheasant and quail . . ."

I'd always wanted to live in the country. A piece of land big enough for the kids and dogs to run, a small garden, an old house in a woodsy setting. Paradise.

At first I had dreaded Jenny's letters. Now I realize it was more self-pity than compassion that made me cry.

She was lonely, having trouble with a neighbor, looking

for a friendly church. "If only you could come now instead of September," she said more than once. "We miss you guys."

I missed her too. Their move had carved a hole out of a lifetime friendship and the wound throbbed. "Joe can't get vacation until September. We'll see you then."

We pulled into their driveway on a Sunday afternoon. Joe and Jack left two hours later for a football game. While the kids chased a huge beachball around the tiny yard, Jenny and I sank into lawn chairs cradling mugs of scalding tea to soothe our already raspy vocal chords.

When she touched my hand and smiled, the light in her eyes could have powered a hundred-watt bulb. "I know you're tired of driving, but Jack took tomorrow off and there's something we'd like you to see."

❈   ❈   ❈

Trees. Hundreds of them swaying gently in a clean crisp breeze; spikes of green against an impossibly wide blue sky. Tall dry grass and thistle weeds going to seed. I felt giddy, drawing in huge draughts of pine-scented air. An apple orchard crouched at one end of an open field. Beyond it, I could just make out the porch and chimney of a huge gray house.

"Ten acres," Jack's arm swept east to west in a long, slow arch. "The house needs a lot of work, but it's livable."

"And it's for sale." Jenny tucked her hand in mine and squeezed.

Jack looked square into Joe's eyes. "How'd you like to own some of this?"

My heart pounded with the rhythm of a flock of geese flying overhead. Their raucous voices blended with my husband's laugh.

"So that's why you wanted to bring us here. Looking for someone to help run the ranch?"

Our friends grinned at each other then turned their smiles on us. "Of course if you're not interested we could contact the Petersons. They've been wanting to get out of the smog for years."

Joe's chuckle bounced off the hills and echoed back to tease my ears. He looked thoughtful then. "Would take some time."

Jack nodded. "We've got until spring."

❊   ❊   ❊

Jack and Jenny built new. Higher up and with a better view. They have a garden and more trees. We have a small patch of woods, a meadow brimming with wildflowers, the apple orchard . . .

At night, when the sun dips into the lake a symphony begins. Crickets sing, bullfrogs drum, moths beat their wings against the screens. By midnight you can throw a stone and hit the stars.

My heart soars. Sometimes God says yes to a dream.

---

1. We will read in this psalm about nature blessing God — about rivers clapping their hands and mountains singing together for joy. Looking through Karen's eyes, what are some of the specific ways she experiences nature blessing God?

The story ends with Karen's heart soaring. How do gratitude and thanksgiving to God cause our hearts to soar?

GOD'S WORD FOR US

Sometimes blessing can mean showing our gratitude to God for his good gifts, and for who he is.
Read Psalm 98.

2. What feelings characterize this psalm?

3. What does this psalm reveal about God?

4. List the specific reasons the psalmist gives for his gratitude to God.

5. What does the psalmist suggest we do to bless God (vv. 4-6)?

6. Have you ever been so full of gratitude to God that you felt like the psalmist did? Describe what you were grateful for.

What did you do to express your gratitude?

_____

7. What do you think it would be like to be as demonstrative in our gratitude and blessing as the psalmist was?

How does it benefit us when we express our gratitude to God?

_____

8. The psalm closes with powerful imagery. What pictures come to mind as you reflect on these verses (7-9)?

_____

9. Make a list of several specific reasons you have for blessing God at this time.

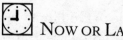 Now or Later

☐ Reread what the psalmist suggest we do to bless God. What could you do to demonstrate your gratitude and joy to God? Let yourself do this.

☐ Write a prayer, blessing God for who he is to you.

☐ Read and reflect on Psalm 100.

6

Blessing Others Through Prayer

Psalm 20

 SETTING THE STAGE:

Irene's Story

Every time I see fresh washed sheets snapping in the wind, I picture Tommy peeking from behind the folds, small teeth flashing white and straight behind his grin. "Betcha can't find me, Grandma Irene."

"Oh, dear, where has Tommy gone? Now where can that boy be?"

He never tired of the game.

Jenny's latest letter says, "We picked blackberries today. Danny couldn't tell the red from black and got a stomachache."

I check the cover on the sandbox, damp from last night's shower, remembering the baby's chubby fists digging, grasping, dropping more sand on the patio than in the pail. The upturned bucket on his head. His wails of pain—"Poor Danny Boy. Let Grandma wipe your eyes."

Protect him, Lord. He's so curious and vulnerable. Protect him from himself.

The letter continues, "Tommy loves his new two-wheeler, but he can't seem to get the hang of the brakes.

He nearly knocked over our elderly neighbor, then finally stopped by running into a tree."

Thank you, Father, that he wasn't hurt. Tommy's so independent. Please give him a hefty dose of common sense.

"We went on an overnight camping trip with the people from Jack's office. They're nice, but most of them drink a lot. I did meet two woman about my age, Alicia and Carol. I think Alicia's a Christian. You know how sometimes you can just tell? I'd like to get to know her better."

I know Jenny's lonely. She doesn't fool me with her everything's-perfect letters. Joyce shares some of hers because she knows I'll pray. *For friends, Lord. A church family.*

And a home of their own, I add when I read the rest.

"Our neighbor's name is Ardice. I'm afraid the boys really bother her, but they need to play outside. It stays light until 10:00, and they don't want to go to sleep."

I find out from Joyce that the neighbor keeps their ball. *Give Jenny wisdom, Lord. These things can get sticky.*

The boys and Jack have been wanting a dog, but a Labrador in a yard that size? I can't blame the neighbor, but she could have been nicer about it. I have to laugh when Jenny says she took chocolate chip cookies as a peace offering. That recipe has soothed more than one prickled spirit over the years.

"She's having headaches, too," Joyce tells me. "The doctor thinks they're migraines."

If I were closer, I could rub her head and take the boys for the afternoon so she could rest.

Oh, Lord, how I long for the sight of them. I know we'll see them at Christmas, but that's such a long way off.

God is so good . . . . We sing that chorus in church and I can't get it out of my head. "It's true, you know." I tell

Joyce. "God is good. Can you believe they finally found that nice piece of land?"

"And their friends are going to buy half. You'd think they would have asked us first."

I knew she was teasing. Joyce would perish living that far from a shopping mall.

"Jenny's dad and I could never manage that much property. But Jenny says there are smaller places on the outskirts of town."

Joyce grins. "We've been talking about moving for years, maybe when the housing market improves."

I smile and picture Tommy running through the knee high grass. "Betcha can't catch me, Grandma Irene."

Oh, yes, Tommy. I bet I can.

---

1. Jenny's mother, Irene, prays for specific blessings for her daughter and grandchildren. What are some of the potential benefits to Jenny, and to Irene, as a result of these prayers?

Think of a time when you prayed for specific blessing for someone, what were the results in that person's life?

in your life?

2. What thoughts and feelings do you have when someone who cares for you prays for you?

 GOD'S WORD FOR US
Read Psalm 20.

3. What thoughts and feelings would you have if someone prayed the words of this psalm for you?

4. Verses 1-5 is an intercessory prayer. List everything the psalmist requests.

Next to each of these requests, write the name of a person you would like to ask God to bless in this way.

5. Included in verse 5 is a statement of anticipation of celebrating God's response of blessing. What is it like for you to have others celebrate with you in this way?

6. What is it like for you to do this with others?

7. The psalmist expresses confidence in God's ability to bless (v. 6). What is the psalmist confident that God will do?

8. It is as if the writer is picturing God responding to his prayer of blessing as he prays. What is helpful about this approach to prayer?

9. What is the basis for your confidence in God's ability and willingness to answer your prayers for others?

Now or Later

☐ Write a psalm of your own, asking for blessing for those you love.

☐ Picture the people you pray for being blessed by God. What images come to mind?

☐ Read and reflect on John 17.

Guidelines for Leaders

My grace is sufficient for you. (2 Corinthians 12:9)

If leading a Bible study is something new for you, don't worry. These studies are designed to be led easily. As a matter of fact, the flow of questions through the passage from observation to interpretation to application is so natural that you may feel that the studies lead themselves.

You don't need to be an expert on the Bible or a trained teacher to lead a Bible discussion. The idea behind these inductive studies is that the leader guides group members to discover for themselves what the Bible has to say. This method of learning will allow group members to remember much more of what is said than a lecture would.

This study guide is flexible. You can use it with a variety of groups—student, professional, neighborhood or church groups. Each study takes about forty-five minutes in a group setting with the possibility of extending the time to sixty minutes or more by adding questions from "Now or Later."

There are some important facts to know about group dynamics and encouraging discussion. The suggestions listed below should enable you to effectively and enjoyably fulfill your role as leader.

Preparing for the Study

1. Ask God to help you understand and apply the passage in your own life. Unless this happens, you will not be prepared to lead others. Pray too for the various members of the group. Ask God to open your hearts to the message of his Word and motivate you to action.

2. Read the introduction to the entire guide to get an overview of the subject at hand and the issues which will be explored. Also read through the introductions to each study to get the flow of the continuing story that runs through the guide and to get familiar with the characters. Be ready to refer the group to the list of characters on the back of the contents page if they have questions about the story.

3. As you begin each study, read and reread the assigned Bible passage to familiarize yourself with it.

4. This study guide is based on the New International Version of the Bible. It will help you and the group if you use this translation as the basis for your study and discussion.

5. Carefully work through each question in the study. Spend time in meditation and reflection as you consider how to respond.

6. Write your thoughts and responses in the space provided in the study guide. This will help you to express your understanding of the passage clearly.

7. It might help you to have a Bible dictionary handy. Use it to look up any unfamiliar words, names or places. (For additional help on how to study a passage, see chapter five of *Leading Bible Discussions*, InterVarsity Press.)

8. Take the "Now or Later" portion of each study seriously. Consider what how you need to apply the

Scripture to your life. Remember that the group will follow your lead in responding to the studies. They will not go any deeper than you do.

Leading the Study

1. Begin the study on time. Open with prayer, asking God to help the group to understand and apply the passage.

2. Be sure that everyone in your group has a study guide. Encourage the group to prepare beforehand for each discussion by reading the introduction to the guide and by working through the questions in the study.

3. At the beginning of your first time together, explain that these studies are meant to be discussions, not lectures. Encourage the members of the group to participate. However, do not put pressure on those who may be hesitant to speak during the first few sessions.

4. Have a group member read the story in "Setting the Stage" at the beginning of the discussion or allow group members some time to read this silently. These stories are designed to draw the readers into the topic of the study and show how the topic is related to our daily lives. It is merely a starting point so don't allow the group members to get bogged down with details of the story or with trying to make a literal connection to the passage to be studied. Just enjoy them.

5. Every study begins with one or more "approach" questions, which are meant to be asked before the passage is read. These questions are designed to connect the opening story with the theme of the study and to encourage group members to begin to open up. Encourage as many members as possible to participate and be ready to get the discussion going with your own response.

Approach questions can reveal where our thoughts or feelings need to be transformed by Scripture. That is why it is especially important not to read the passage before the approach question is asked. The passage will tend to color the honest reactions people would otherwise give because they are, of course, supposed to think the way the Bible does.

6. Have a group member read aloud the passage to be studied.

7. As you ask the questions under "God's Word for Us," keep in mind that they are designed to be used just as they are written. You may simply read them aloud. Or you may prefer to express them in your own words.

There may be times when it is appropriate to deviate from the study guide. For example, a question may have already been answered. If so, move on to the next question. Or someone may raise an important question not covered in the guide. Take time to discuss it, but try to keep the group from going off on tangents.

8. Avoid answering your own questions. If necessary, repeat or rephrase them until they are clearly understood. An eager group quickly becomes passive and silent if they think the leader will do most of the talking.

9. Don't be afraid of silence. People may need time to think about the question before formulating their answers.

10. Don't be content with just one answer. Ask, "What do the rest of you think?" or "Anything else?" until several people have given answers to the question.

11. Acknowledge all contributions. Try to be affirming whenever possible. Never reject an answer. If it is clearly off-base, ask, "Which verse led you to that conclusion?" or again, "What do the rest of you think?"

12. Don't expect every answer to be addressed to you,

even though this will probably happen at first. As group members become more at ease, they will begin to truly interact with each other. This is one sign of healthy discussion.

13. Don't be afraid of controversy. It can be very stimulating. If you don't resolve an issue completely, don't be frustrated. Move on and keep it in mind for later. A subsequent study may solve the problem.

14. Periodically summarize what the group has said about the passage. This helps to draw together the various ideas mentioned and gives continuity to the study. But don't preach.

15. "Now or Later" can be used in a variety of ways depending on the time available to you and the interests of your group members. You may want to discuss an application question or idea and make some commitments. Or you may want to allow five minutes or so of quiet reflection within the group time so that people can journal their responses. Then, ask simply, "What did you experience (and/or learn) as you journaled?"

You will want to use at least one of these ideas to wrap up the group time, but you may want to encourage group members to continue working through other ideas throughout the week. You can continue discussing what has been learned at your next meeting.

16. Conclude your time together with conversational prayer. Ask for God in following through on the commitments you've made.

17. End on time.

Many more suggestions and helps are found in *Small Group Leaders' Handbook* and *The Big Book on Small Groups* (both from InterVarsity Press). Reading through one of these books would be worth your time.

Study Notes

Study 1. Called to Be Blessed and to Be a Blessing. Genesis 12:1-5.

Purpose: To explore ways God blesses us and uses us to bless others.

Question 2. God makes several promises to Abram. He promises to make him into a great nation, to make his name great, to bless him, to make him a blessing, to bless those who bless him, to curse those who curse him and to bless all the people of the earth through him. Abram is later renamed by God as "Abraham" (see Genesis 17:1-8) when God announces that he will be called "the father of the nations."

Question 3. God asked Abram to leave his country, his people and his father's household and to go to a land which God had yet to show him. In the late twentieth century the request to leave country and family may not seem too extreme. We are a population of immigrants and live in a world connected by the internet, satellites and jets. And we are a culture which values independence from parents. Moving thousands of miles away from family is the norm.

But for Abram things were different. There were no

jets or internet, there wasn't even a pony express mail service. And sons were not to leave their people or their father's household. Abraham lived in a patriachical culture where sons stayed within the father's household. To leave was to break family and cultural rules. To leave was to be without communication, without contact or connection. To leave under these circumstances and not know where you were going would have been seen as bordering on lunacy. God was asking a lot of Abram.

Question 4. Blessings that are simply given to us without our active participation are many. The air we breathe, the moment-by-moment functioning of our body's complex systems, the sun which warms us, the oceans which cool the earth, the beauty of creation—the list is endless.

Question 5. Consider the many ways we actively participate with God in his blessing of us. This might include our work, actively showing love to someone else or our obedience to specific guidance in big and little decisions.

Question 7. The benefits of our active participation in receiving God's blessing is that our participation changes us. Our relationship with God deepens, our faith grows, our sense of being in a vital relationship with God grows, our sense of being valued by God as coparticipants in his work increases.

Question 8. People of the earth have been blessed by Abram (Abraham) through the law, the covenant, the prophets, the apostles and through Christ. God chose to use Abram's descendants to communicate his passionate love for all people.

Question 9. The relationship between being blessed by God and being a blessing is somewhat like the relationship of the sun's light shining on the moon and the moon reflecting it. It is the relationship between knowing you are deeply loved and being able to deeply love others. It is the relationship between receiving abundantly from God (materially, spiritually) and sharing that abundance with others.

Now or Later. These are further activities and exercises on the theme of the study. If you are studying on your own, you may want to try several of these ideas in your quiet times after you have done the study. If you are leading a group, you may want to use one of these ideas to close the meeting. You can also encourage group members to try some of these during the week, and then discuss them at the beginning of the next meeting.

Study 2. Receiving Blessing from God. Psalm 84.

Purpose: To explore the blessings which come from an intimate relationship with God.

Question 2. The psalmist describes his experience of God's presence as "lovely." He goes on to write that even the sparrow and the swallow have made homes near the altar, and people who live in God's house and do nothing but praise God are blessed.

For the second part of this question, if you are leading a group, encourage people to share whatever may be true for them. Like David, we may often experience a strong sense of God's presence when we are with other believers and are focused on God, as in times of worship. But the experience of God's presence is not limited to places of worship. Some may experience God while talking with a friend or praying with a small group; they may experience him during times of meditation; they may experience him when at the beach or in the woods; they may experience his presence while driving to work, or while in the shower, or while doing dishes or working in the yard.

Question 3. The author's experience of being away from God's presence is the experience of a lover being away from his beloved. He writes of his "soul yearning, even fainting," and of his "heart and flesh crying out for the living God."

Question 4. The metaphor of finding strength in God, might be seen as a picture of depending on God. The metaphor of setting one's heart on a pilgrimage, might be seen as a picture of being single-minded about wanting to live in close relationship with God. If you are leading a group, encourage members to offer a variety of thoughts about these two metaphors.

Question 5. The blessings that are promised continue the metaphor of being on a pilgrimage: (1) as they pass through the Valley of Baca, they will make it a place of springs and it will be covered with pools (the Valley of Baca is translated by some as "the parched valley"), and (2) they will go from strength to strength until each pilgrim appears before God. These metaphors are promises of blessings of abundant provision and personal growth.

Question 6. If you are in a group, allow a few minutes of silence for each person to write a prayer on a piece of paper or in her study guide. Then ask, "What did you experience in writing this prayer?" Give group members permission to be general or specific according to their comfort level.

Question 7. The writer describes God as someone who is wonderful to be close to. He describes God as a sun and shield, and a generous giver of all good things.

Question 8. If you are leading a group, remind the members of the reality that was discussed in the first study — (1) we are asked by God to be active participants in a relationship with him, and (2) it is out of that relationship that we experience God's richest blessings. Encourage group members to talk about how they have experienced this themselves.

Study 3. Receiving Blessing from God's Family. Ephesians 4:1-16.

Purpose: To provide an opportunity to examine how God uses others to bless our lives.

Question 2. Paul encourages us to be humble, gentle, patient, forbearing (forgiving or full-of-grace) and loving. These qualities are Christlike. They characterize the way Christ is toward us.

These qualities in a person allow them to be a healing influence because we feel safe, valued, respected, loved, free to be honest and able to be our true selves with a person who has these qualities. It is in this kind of an environment that we change, grow and heal.

Question 3. Encourage group members to talk about their experiences of being spiritually and emotionally connected to other believers, and how these experiences were helpful (a blessing) to them.

Question 4. If you are leading a group, encourage members to describe experiences when they have not felt this kind of closeness or belonging and to discuss whatever difficulties this might have created for them. Summarize these discussions by highlighting our need for support and love (blessing) from other members of God's family.

Question 5. Consider what it was about the specific ministry of another Christian that was especially helpful to you.

Question 6. Paul uses the metaphors of infants and the metaphor of a human body which is growing and developing. He describes our need for stability, which is met when we are "held together" and "supported" by close connection with other parts of the body of Christ.

Question 7. The benefits (blessing) we can have in each other's lives include providing stability, maturity, belonging, love.

Question 8. Knowing that we are loved provides the fertile ground for spiritual growth because when we know that we are loved we are free to take an honest look at ourselves. We are free to change the things that need changing. We are free to express and be who we really are. We have increased faith and hope in our own value and potential. We have a strong desire to be like the one who loves us—that is, to be loving and compassionate toward ourselves and toward others.

Study 4. Being a Blessing to Others. Philippians 4:1-9.

Purpose: To discover how we can bless others.

Question 2. Paul calls the believers in Phillipi "dear friends," (v. 1) and "brothers" (vv. 1 and 8) who are his "joy" and "crown." He tells them that he loves them and that he longs for them (misses them, has deep feelings for them). Paul has intimate knowledge of their relationships and is willing to address a difficult problem in their midst (vv. 2-3). Paul directly addresses them in an affirming, passionate way. Paul has spent much time with them and can serve as a model for them (v. 9).

Question 3. Consider how you might feel if someone you loved and who had been a significant source of spiritual blessing to you wrote a letter which addressed you in this way.

Question 4. Paul begins by pleading with Euodia and Syntyche to resolve the conflict they are having. He urges the other believers to help them and support them and to value them as he does, as women who have worked side-by-side with him.

Paul also encourages the believers to rejoice, to find joy in the Lord—in his love and goodness. And he encourages them to be gentle (compassionate, respectful, loving, patient) in their interactions with everyone they have dealings with.

Question 5. If you are in a group, discuss how resolving conflicts and supporting others in the process of conflict resolution brings blessing (including reconciliation, peace and love) and how finding joy in the Lord and being gentle in interactions with others brings blessing.

Question 6. Encourage group members to speak honestly about their struggles to resolve conflicts, to find joy in their relationship with the Lord, and to be gentle in their interactions with others.

Growth in our ability to resolve conflicts or to rejoice in the Lord or to be gentle in our interactions with others might come from a variety of sources. Allow participants to share things that have been helpful to them so that they can glean from each other's experiences of growth in these areas.

Question 7. The behaviors that lead to being at peace, according to this text include making everything that causes us anxiety a subject of prayer, presenting our requests to God, giving thanks, and reflecting (meditating) on whatever is noble, right, pure, lovely, admirable, excellent, praiseworthy.

This requires us to pay attention to our reactions so that we are aware that we are anxious when we are anxious. This is not always easy to figure out because sometimes we hide our anxiety behind trying to control other people's behavior, becoming angry, or blaming. Or we might hide our anxiety by withdrawing emotionally or spiritually or physically from others. It is helpful to have some idea of how we hide our anxiety and what things are likely to make us anxious, so we can more readily realize and acknowledge our anxiety to ourselves and to God.

Once we realize that we are anxious, we need to release our anxiety and the event or person we are anxious about into God's loving care. We need to talk to God about what is troubling us and what we need.

In the midst of this process we are to give thanks. That is, we are to acknowledge who God is and what he has done for us in the past. This helps us remember his love and faithfulness, and helps us to trust him with the things that trouble us.

Finally, we are to turn our minds to things that inspire hope and courage and faithfulness.

This is a process we may need to repeat many times a day. **Question 8.** Think of people who are at peace and reflect on ways their peacefulness blesses you. When we are at peace, we are less likely to be trying to control other people or to be blaming other people, and we are more likely to listen to and respect and respond to other people's needs and concerns.

Study 5. Blessing God Through Thanksgiving. Psalm 98.

Purpose: To discover the joy of returning blessing to God through gratitude and praise.

Question 2. The feelings expressed directly or indirectly in this psalm include feelings of gratitude, hope, joy, love, adoration and excitement.

Question 3. This psalm reveals that God is powerful, that he does marvelous things, that he is righteous, that he is a saving God, that he is loving and faithful, that he is the judge of the earth and will judge with fairness.

Question 4. The psalmist is grateful to God because God has remembered his love and his commitment to Israel and has provided salvation for them, and in so doing, has revealed his power and his character to all the peoples of the earth.

Question 5. The psalmist suggests that we sing a new song to the Lord, that we shout for joy, that we burst into jubilant song, that we make music with a harp and trumpets and horns.

Question 6. Describe times of great joy or deep gratitude.

Question 7. Expressing our joy and gratitude with abandon, as the psalmist suggests might feel energizing and even fun. Joy is a visceral emotion, it can make us feel like "bursting." When we express our joy and gratitude with our bodies and voices, we do not have to contain it or suppress it, and as a result, we can feel it more fully.

Question 8. The imagery of the last verses includes images of the sea and every living thing in the world resounding (respond back to God), the rivers clapping their hands, and the mountains singing together in joy. If you are leading a group, encourage members to describe the specific pictures that come to mind as they reflect on all of nature responding to God in joy.

Study 6. Blessing Others Through Prayer. Psalm 20.

Purpose: To allow participants to explore ways they can pray for God's blessing for others.

Question 2. In a group talk about experiences of having someone pray for you, especially for your healing or protection of blessing. Often the experience of being loved and valued is very profound in these situations.

Question 3. The experience of having someone pray this powerful blessing might include feelings of being cherished and deeply cared for. It would be an experience of someone asking God to give you the very best of everything.

Question 4. The purpose of this exercise is to think in terms of praying for specific blessing for people you know. If you are leading a group, ask members how they felt about making this list.

Question 5. The psalmist anticipates great things to happen, and says that when it does, he will rejoice with the person being blessed. Sharing another person's joy in this way multiplies the joy many times over. Experiencing success or victory without anyone to celebrate with can be an empty thing. But experiencing success or victory with others reflecting our joy and being genuinely happy for us is an experience of being loved and valued.

Question 6. Encourage group members to talk about the difficulties and the rewards of sharing in other people's successes and joy. It might be useful to talk about what can make this a difficult thing to do, and what might make it possible.

Question 7. The psalmist says that he is confident ("I know," v. 6) that the Lord saves his anointed and answers him with saving power.

Question 8. Picturing God responding to our requests for blessing can build our faith and hope. It can help us to wait with anticipation and grow in our trust of God's intimate love and care for all people.

Question 9. Reflect on who God is and on how you have seen God care for you and for others in the past.

Other Bible Studies by Juanita Ryan

Women of Character Bible Studies
A Woman of Balance
A Woman of Beauty
A Woman of Blessing
A Woman of Confidence

LifeGuide® Bible Studies
Psalms II

Life Recovery Guides by Juanita and Dale Ryan
Recovery: A Lifelong Journey
Recovery from Abuse
Recovery from Addictions
Recovery from Bitterness
Recovery from Broken Relationships
Recovery from Codependency
Recovery from Depression
Recovery from Distorted Images of God
Recovery from Distorted Images of Self
Recovery from Family Dysfunctions
Recovery from Fear
Recovery from Guilt
Recovery from Loss
Recovery from Shame
Recovery from Spiritual Abuse
Recovery from Workaholism

Novels by Linda Shands

Seasons Remembered Series
A Time to Keep
A Time to Embrace
A Time to Search
A Time to Speak